# TAPESTRIES

## STORIES OF WOMEN
## IN THE BIBLE

RETOLD AND ILLUSTRATED BY
# RUTH SANDERSON

Little, Brown and Company

Boston   New York   Toronto   London

First Edition
The source for these stories is the
Revised Standard Version of the Bible.

Library of Congress Cataloging-in-Publication Data

Sanderson, Ruth.
    Tapestries : stories of women in the Bible / retold and illustrated
by Ruth Sanderson. —1st ed.
        p.   cm.
    Summary: Presents twenty-three stories about women in the Old
and New Testaments, including Eve, Rebekah, and Ruth.
    ISBN 0-316-77093-0
    1. Women in the Bible—Juvenile literature.   2. Bible stories,
English. [1.Women in the Bible.  2.Bible stories.]  I. Title.
BS575.S324  1998
220.9'2' '082—dc21
    [B]                                                                97-6319

10  9  8  7  6  5  4  3  2  1
SC
Published simultaneously in Canada by
Little, Brown & Company (Canada) Limited

Printed in Hong Kong

# THE OLD TESTAMENT

# EVE

Adam and Eve were the first man and woman created by God. They lived in a lush garden paradise called Eden, filled with many trees laden with delicious fruits. In the center of the garden, next to a stream, grew two trees that were different from the others. One was the Tree of Knowledge of good and evil. Adam and Eve were forbidden by God to eat the fruit from that tree.

One day a serpent spoke to Eve, saying, "If you eat the fruit of this tree, you will not die, but rather you will be like God, knowing good and evil."

Eve was fooled by the serpent's words. Desiring to be wise, she ate some of the fruit and gave some to Adam. Immediately they knew they had been wrong to disobey God. Ashamed and afraid, they hid themselves.

Adam and Eve were banished from the Garden of Eden. God sent an angel with a flaming sword to guard the way back to the garden, for He did not want them to eat the fruit of the Tree of Life lest they live forever in their misery.

Adam labored and tilled the land to grow their food, and Eve bore him many children, of whom Cain and Abel were the first and second. Eve showed her respect for God when she gave birth to her first son and said, "I have gotten a man with the help of the Lord."

# SARAH

Sarah was married to Abraham, a good man who was favored by God. When they were very old, the Lord appeared to them in the form of three men. Abraham fetched food and drink while the men sat in the shade of a great oak tree.

"Where is Sarah, your wife?" they asked.

"She is in the tent," replied Abraham.

"I will return in the spring, and Sarah, your wife, shall have a son," said one of the men.

Now, Sarah was listening from behind the tent flap and laughed to herself at the idea of a woman her age having a baby. She was over ninety years old! And yet a year later she gave birth to a son, whom they named Isaac.

"God has made me laugh," said Sarah, "so that everyone who hears my story will laugh, too." Abraham was one hundred years old when his son was born.

"Sarah shall be a mother of nations," said the Lord to Abraham. "Kings of people shall come from her."

# REBEKAH

When Sarah's son, Isaac, was old enough to marry, his father, Abraham, sent his faithful servant to Sarah and Abraham's homeland to find a wife for him. After a long journey, the servant arrived at a well outside the city of Nahor. The servant prayed to God that the maiden who would come to the well and offer water to him and his camels would be the one whom God had chosen for Isaac. Right after he finished praying, a beautiful maiden with a water jug on her shoulder came to the well.

"Drink, my lord," she said when he asked her for water, "and I will also draw water for your camels."

The servant gave her a golden nose-ring and golden bracelets. He asked her name, and praised God when she replied that she was Rebekah, daughter of Abraham's nephew Bethuel. He visited her home and explained his task. Rebekah agreed to become Isaac's wife. Rebekah and Isaac married soon after and lived very happily together.

# MIRIAM

At the time Miriam's brother Moses was born, the Jewish people were oppressed by the Pharaoh, who decreed that all Jewish boy babies were to be drowned. Moses' mother hid him so that Pharaoh's men would not put him to death.

When Moses was three months old, his mother made a cradle of reeds and put him in it. She laid it in the bulrushes by the river and told his sister Miriam to watch it. Soon after, Pharaoh's daughter came down to the river with her servants, and hearing a baby crying, sent her maid to fetch him. The princess felt sorry for the baby and decided that she would bring him up as her own son. Miriam, thinking quickly, approached the princess and asked if she would like a nurse for him from the Hebrew women. When she agreed, Miriam ran home and brought back the baby's own mother, and the princess paid her to care for the child.

Miriam's act allowed Moses to be raised by his own mother, after which he was sent to the princess and educated by the Egyptians. Miriam grew up to be a prophet and a leader of the women during the Jews' Exodus from Egypt.

# Rahab

When Joshua, the leader of the Israelites after Moses, was told by God to take possession of the beautiful land of Canaan, he sent two spies to the city of Jericho to gather information. The spies lodged at the house of a woman named Rahab. She had heard of the miraculous passage of the Israelites through the Red Sea, and she believed that the God of Israel was the one true God.

It became known to the king of that land that the spies were there, and he sent officers to arrest them. But Rahab saw them coming. She hid the spies on her roof under stalks of flax. When the officers left, she went back to the spies. They promised her that when Joshua took the city, she and her family would be spared.

Rahab's house was at the city wall. She let the spies down by a scarlet cord, and they escaped to the mountains and back to their leader, Joshua. In the battle that followed, Rahab and her family were not harmed.

# DEBORAH

Deborah was a judge and prophetess for the people of Israel when they were slaves to King Jabin of Hazor.

Deborah summoned a man named Barak and said, "The Lord commands you to gather your men at Mount Tabor. I will draw out Sisera, the general of Jabin's army, with his troops, and I will deliver them into your hands."

Barak said to her, "If you go with me, I will go."

And Deborah fearlessly agreed to go into battle, saying, "I will surely go with you." Then she added prophetically, "But that road will not lead to your glory, for the Lord will sell Sisera into the hands of a woman."

# JAEL

When Sisera's army was defeated by the army led by Barak and Deborah, Sisera escaped on foot. He fled to the tent of Jael, whose husband was at peace with King Jabin.

"Have no fear," Jael said to Sisera. She led him into her tent and covered him with a rug. When he asked for water, she gave him milk. Then, when Sisera fell asleep, she took a tent peg and a hammer and drove it into his head, and so he died.

Later that day, Deborah sang a song of victory, praising the daring of Jael, who had risked her life to help the Israelites.

# RUTH

A man and his wife, Naomi, left their home in Bethlehem during a famine and went to live in the country of Moab. Their son married a Moabite named Ruth. Both Ruth's husband and Naomi's husband died a few years later, leaving them widows.

Naomi heard that the famine was over, and she decided to return to Bethlehem. Ruth insisted on going with her, saying, "Your people shall be my people and your God my God."

They arrived in Bethlehem during the barley harvest. A kinsman of Naomi's husband owned a large field. His name was Boaz.

Ruth said to Naomi, "Let me go into the field to glean, and perhaps I will find favor in your kinsman's sight."

When Boaz came by at the end of the day, he noticed Ruth and asked his servant about her. After learning her story, he went to Ruth and said, "Glean close to my maidens, and when you are thirsty, drink from their vessels."

When Ruth asked why he would show such favor to a foreigner, he replied, "I have learned what you have done for your mother-in-law, Naomi. You left your own father and mother and your native land and came to a people that you did not know. The Lord will reward you for what you have done." Boaz later told his men to leave extra sheaves on the ground so that Ruth would find plenty of grain to glean. Naomi rejoiced when Ruth came home with so much bounty, and she knew that their troubles were past.

Soon after, Boaz took Ruth for his wife, and Naomi became nurse to their son Obed. And Obed was father to Jesse, the father of David.

# HANNAH

Hannah lived with her husband on Mount Ephraim. One day she went into the Temple and prayed to God to give her a little boy, for she had no children. She vowed that if He granted her prayer, she would devote the child to His service. Soon after, Hannah had a son and called him Samuel. When he was old enough, Hannah took her son to the Temple and dedicated him to the Lord. He stayed there with Eli the high priest and waited on him and helped him at the altar. Every year Hannah visited Samuel, bringing him a fine new robe that she made with her own hands.

# THE WITCH OF ENDOR

When Samuel grew up, he became a great prophet. He was adviser to King Saul, a weak and foolish ruler who often did not heed Samuel's words. After Samuel died, King Saul was lost without his advice. The Philistines waged war against him, and he did not know what to do. Although it was forbidden, in desperation, he sought out a witch to call back spirits from the dead.

"Bring up Samuel for me!" commanded King Saul. The Witch of Endor obeyed, and the spirit of Samuel stood before them. But the king was not comforted by his words. "You have disobeyed God," said the ghost, "and tomorrow you and your sons shall be with me, and the Lord shall give the army of Israel into the hands of the Philistines."

Then the witch took pity on King Saul, who had fallen to the floor when the spirit departed. She gave him bread and had a fatted calf cooked for him. The next day Saul met his death upon the battlefield, as Samuel had foretold.

# ABIGAIL

Abigail was the wife of a very rich man named Nabal, who was known to be rude and ill-mannered. He owned three thousand sheep and a thousand goats. One day, ten soldiers came to him from David's army, begging for supplies in David's name. Nabal offered them insults instead of food. When David heard of this, he became enraged, for his soldiers had protected Nabal's shepherds in the wilderness.

"Every man put on his sword!" he commanded. Four hundred men were soon armed and ready to take vengeance against Nabal for his insult to David.

Luckily, a servant told Abigail how rudely her husband had refused David's men. Immediately, Abigail gathered together two hundred loaves, wine, the meat of five sheep, grain, one hundred clusters of raisins, and two hundred cakes of figs. Her men packed all these things on mules, and without telling her husband, Abigail herself went with the caravan to David's camp. She begged him to disregard her ill-natured husband and accept her gifts instead.

"Blessed be the Lord God of Israel, who sent you this day to meet me," said David to Abigail. "For you have kept me this day from blood guilt!" And David accepted her gifts of food and sent her back to her home in peace.

Soon after, Nabal died. David heard this news and remembered the brave and beautiful Abigail. He sent word to Abigail and asked her to marry him. And so Abigail became the wife of David.

# BATHSHEBA

David became King of Israel after Saul. He was a great and good king. He was also human, and sometimes he did things that were wrong.

One day King David saw a beautiful woman from his palace window. He was so struck by her beauty that he wanted her for his wife. But when he asked about her, he learned that she was already married, to a soldier named Uriah. David came up with a plan to do away with Uriah, for he was so in love with Bathsheba that nothing could stop his desire to have her for himself.

David sent a message to Uriah's commander, telling him to send Uriah into the front lines of the next battle. When the commander did as the king ordered, Uriah was killed.

After a time of mourning for her dead husband, Bathsheba married King David and bore him a son. God did not let David go unpunished for his crime. He was visited by the prophet Nathan, who told the king that his son would die, and so it was. In time Bathsheba gave birth to another son, Solomon. He became king after David and built the great Temple at Jerusalem.

# THE QUEEN OF SHEBA

The Queen of Sheba was captivated by tales of Solomon's riches and great wisdom, both of which reportedly equaled her own. The queen had a caravan loaded with treasure and went to see for herself and to test this Solomon.

Solomon answered all her riddles, and his great treasure houses made her feel poor. "Your wisdom and wealth surpass the reports that I have heard," she told him. "Because the Lord loves Israel, He has made you king." And the Queen of Sheba gave Solomon many gifts: gold and spices, precious stones, and musical instruments. King Solomon then let the queen pick all that she wanted from his own treasure before she returned to her homeland in Arabia.

# The
# New Testament

Mary of Nazareth

Elizabeth

Anna

Mary and Martha

Procula

Mary Magdalene

Lydia

Priscilla

Phoebe

Tabitha

# MARY OF NAZARETH

Joachim and Anna, descendants of the house of David, longed for a child. Finally their prayers were answered, and Anna gave birth to a girl, named Mary.

When Mary came of age, she was betrothed to a man named Joseph, a carpenter by trade. In June of that year, the angel Gabriel appeared to Mary, saying, "Hail, favored one. The Lord is with you." Mary was confused by this greeting and frightened at the angel's awesome appearance.

"Do not be afraid, for you have found favor with God," Gabriel reassured her. "Behold, you will conceive in your womb and bear a son, and you shall call his name Jesus. He will be great, He will be called the son of the Most High, and of His kingdom there will be no end."

Then Mary said to the angel, "How shall this be, since I have no husband yet?"

Gabriel replied, "The Holy Spirit will come upon you, and therefore the child to be born will be called holy, the Son of God." He went on to tell her, "Your kinswoman Elizabeth, in her old age, has also conceived a son, because with God nothing is impossible."

And Mary said to the angel Gabriel, "Behold, I am the handmaid of the Lord. Let it be to me according to your word."

# ELIZABETH

Mary's cousin Elizabeth lived with her husband, Zachariah, in the hill country of Judea. They, too, were visited by an angel bearing strange news. He told them that a son was to be born to Elizabeth, though she was old and barren.

"You shall call his name John, and he will be filled with the Holy Spirit even from his mother's womb," said the angel. "And he will make ready for the Lord a people prepared."

When Mary went to visit Elizabeth, she greeted her warmly. Suddenly Elizabeth felt the baby leap in her womb. She was filled with the Holy Spirit and declared to Mary, "Blessed are you among women, and blessed is the fruit of your womb!"

Mary stayed with Elizabeth for three months, then returned to her home in Nazareth. When her time came, Elizabeth gave birth to a son and he was named John. John grew up to become a great prophet, known as John the Baptist.

# ANNA

According to custom, a number of days after the birth of Jesus, Mary and Joseph brought him to the Temple, to present him to the Lord, bringing with them a sacrifice of two turtledoves. The devout man Simeon met them, and the prophetess Anna was there at the same hour. She had spent her life in worship, fasting, and prayer. Anna recognized this small baby as the Savior and joyfully gave thanks to God. Afterward, she told many people about Jesus, who was to be the redeemer of Jerusalem.

# MARY AND MARTHA

Mary and Martha were two sisters who lived in the town of Bethany. Their table was always set for travelers and friends passing by. Jesus was well known by them, and one day he came to supper at their house. Martha bustled about, busily preparing and serving the food and drink. Mary, however, sat at the feet of Jesus and listened closely to all he said.

Martha grew annoyed that she was doing all the work by herself. "Lord, tell my sister to help me," she said to Jesus.

"Martha, Martha," he replied, "you are anxious and troubled about many things. One thing is needful. Mary has chosen the good portion, which shall not be taken from her."

# PROCULA

Procula was the wife of Pontius Pilate, the governor who had Jesus arrested. The morning that her husband was sitting in judgment of Jesus, she sent a message to him, saying she had had a dream about Jesus that had greatly troubled her. She urged Pilate to have nothing to do with Jesus, for she knew he was a righteous man. That day, Pilate told the crowd he would release one prisoner. He gave them the choice of Jesus or the thief Barabbas, hoping they would choose to free Jesus. But it was not to be so. The crowd chose Barabbas, and Jesus was crucified.

# Mary Magdalene

Mary of Magdalene was a devoted follower of Jesus. She stood by, weeping with Mary, the mother of Jesus, as he died on the cross. She watched as he was laid in a new tomb, and she saw the great stone rolled in front of the entrance to seal the tomb.

At dawn on the first day of the week, Mary went to the tomb with spices to anoint the body of Jesus. There was a great quaking of the earth, and an angel of the Lord appeared and rolled away the stone. The angel was radiant, and his garments were as white as snow. He spoke to Mary: "Do not be afraid, for I know you seek Jesus, who was crucified. He is not here, for He is risen. Come and see the place where He did lay." Mary did as the angel said, and when she saw that the tomb was indeed empty, the angel continued, "Go quickly and tell the other disciples that He has risen from the dead and that He will meet with you soon in Galilee."

As Mary ran to tell the disciples this amazing news, Jesus himself appeared to her. Mary recognized who He was, and fell at His feet with joy. "Mary," said Jesus, "tell my brothers I am ascending to my Father and to your Father, to my God and your God."

"I have seen the Lord!" declared Mary to the disciples, and she told them all that had happened.

# LYDIA

In the early days after Jesus' death and resurrection, the apostles traveled far and wide, spreading His Gospels and teachings. Drawn by a vision, the apostles Paul and Silas went to Philippi, in Macedonia. There they held a prayer meeting by the riverside. Among the women in attendance was a merchant named Lydia. She was quite wealthy, as her trade goods were the finely woven silks bought by the ruling class. When Paul spoke, her heart was opened and she became a believer. After she was baptized along with the members of her household, Lydia invited the apostles to spend the night at her house, saying, "If you have judged me to be faithful to the Lord, come to my house and stay."

# PRISCILLA

Priscilla and her husband, Aquila, were tent makers by trade. They traveled far and wide, living in a tent themselves and selling their tents in many places. The apostle Paul visited them in Corinth, Ephesus, and Rome. Paul preached sermons in their home and often sewed tents with them as well. Paul's letter to the Romans begins, "Aquila and Priscilla salute you in the Lord, with the church that is in their home." On more than one occasion, Priscilla and her husband risked their lives for Paul's sake. For depending on who was ruling at the time, the preaching of Christianity was often forbidden.

# PHOEBE

As the apostles could not be everywhere at all times, they continued to teach people who had converted to Christianity by sending letters. One of Paul's letters to the Romans was delivered by a woman named Phoebe. By carrying the letter, she risked her life, for if caught, she might have been put to death. In his letter, Paul says: "I commend to you our sister Phoebe, a deacon of the church, so that you may welcome her in the Lord as befits the saints, and help her in whatever she may need, for she has helped many and has been a helper to me as well."

# TABITHA

When the apostle Peter was preaching at Lydda, two men from Joppa sought him out and told him that Tabitha was dead. Peter knew Tabitha well. She had made clothing for widows and for the poor for many years. Peter rushed to her house in Joppa, where she was lying in state, surrounded by the many people she had helped. Weeping, they showed Peter the many tunics and garments she had made for them. Peter sent them from the room. He knelt to pray, then turning to the body, he said, "Tabitha, rise!" She opened her eyes, and seeing Peter, she reached out her hand, and he helped her to her feet. When the people of Joppa heard of this miracle, many believed in the Lord.

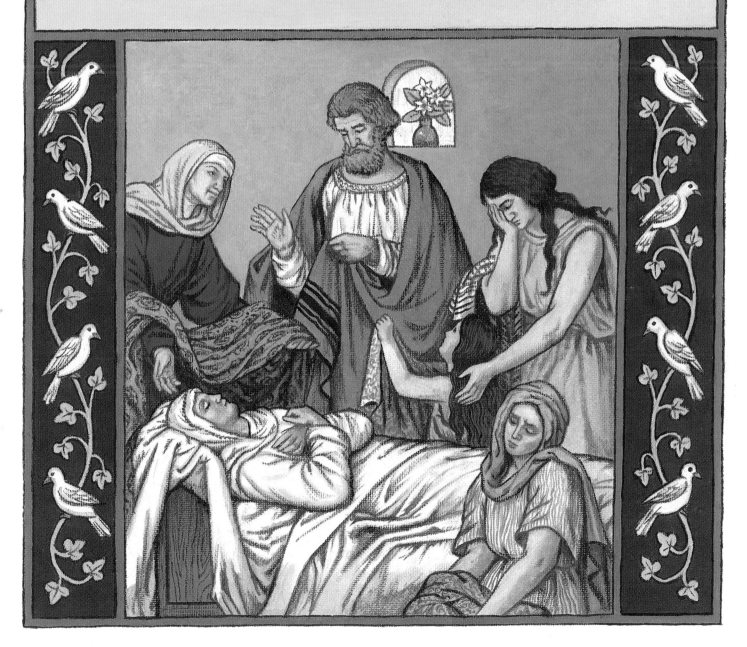

# Author's Note

I have always loved the look and feel of tapestries, beautiful decorative pictures woven into cloth. For the images and portraits in this book, I have used oil paint instead of thread and tried to achieve that same rich look and texture. I have tried to weave the stories of these women with words and with pictures into a tapestry of many colors, elaborate in detail.

Throughout the ages, women have traditionally been in charge of the important tasks of spinning, weaving, and sewing. Some of the women in these stories used needle and thread to profess their faith, while others used a more symbolic weaving in their lives.

The Witch of Endor wove a spell for Saul. Rahab used a scarlet cord to help two spies escape capture. Priscilla sewed tents, and Lydia was a merchant of richly woven silk. The cradle of reeds woven by the mother of Moses saved him from the Pharaoh's men.

Some of the women portrayed in this book take up just a few threads, as they are mentioned only briefly in the Bible. But by examining their stories closely, we appreciate their beauty and recognize their contributions to the greater tapestry into which their lives are woven. It is a tapestry that is more than two thousand years long and continues to be woven to this day.